LEON TROTS

A Life From Beginning to End

Copyright © 2017 by Hourly History.

Table of Contents

Introduction

It was 1919, and the man known as Leon Trotsky was on a train, about to arrive at its destination. It was not only a physical destination that he was racing toward but also an ideological one. He sat in barely constrained anticipation as his train car tore a path through the Ukraine toward his ultimate goal, the goal he had been striving for most of his life: post-revolutionary Russia.

The tsar had already been overthrown, but yet the war still raged between the so-called White Armies that still claimed to support the deposed leader, and the Red Army of the communist Soviets. But by the time of Trotsky's arrival on the scene, the tide had turned dramatically in favor of the Soviets, and the defeat of their White Army opposition was all but assured.

The enigmatic socialist thinker, as he stared absentmindedly out his window, tightly clutched the railing of his seat and was not all that concerned with Russia's impending recent victory, however. He was more interested in what should be done next. Trotsky mind was always one step ahead of his peers.

Unlike the men who would supplant him, such as Lenin and Stalin, he did not subscribe to the notion that the Soviets should take a moment to catch their breath and consolidate their hold on power. Trotsky believed that they needed to seize the moment and advance toward what he considered the ultimate goal of Marxism: worldwide revolution.

In his philosophical meanderings, he insisted on nothing short of a global revolution that would free the entire planet from the "evils of capitalism." He envisioned that this revolution would bring forth a universal communist society, free of borders, class structures, and elitists, whether they be tsars, kings, dictators, or presidents.

For Trotsky, all of the above-mentioned distinctions were just another name for the greedy landlords who wanted to unnaturally create class distinctions, national boundaries, and other artificial walls of separation between a humanity that should be united as one. He mused all of these thoughts as his train pulled into the station, and he had his assistant who was seated nearby write down his words.

He quietly dictated, "A cavalry corps of 30 to 40,000 horsemen must be formed to invade India. The path to Paris and London lies through the cities of Afghanistan, the Punjab, and Bengal. Our victories in the Urals and Siberia must greatly raise the prestige of the Soviet Republic throughout oppressed Asia."

That day on the train, Trotsky was speaking of—among other things—an invasion of Afghanistan. He firmly believed that if he could gather some of the more downtrodden and oppressed nations of the east under the banner of Soviet communism, he would be able to build a power base that would be unbreakable by the west.

And in doing so, he would have added millions of grateful and fanatic believers to the cause, fighting for the future liberation of Europe from the industrialists that

Trotsky believed to be holding them down. And inevitably after the fall of Europe, the United States and the rest of the world would follow. As Trotsky's train came to a stop at its station and his own train of thought came to a close, he was thinking of outright world domination.

Chapter One

How Trotsky Became Trotsky

"The depth and strength of a human character are defined by its moral reserves; people reveal themselves completely when they are thrown out of the customary conditions of their life, for only then do they have to fall back on their reserves."

—Leon Trotsky

Leon Trotsky was born with the name Lev Davidovich Bronstein to his mother Anna Bronstein and his father David Bronstein, on November 7, 1879. The Bronsteins were farmers in the Ukrainian village of Yanovka. Trotsky's father David was a self-made man, who had moved to the region with next to no farming experience. After three decades of his relentless hard labor and sheer ingenuity, David had become one of the most successful farmers in the region, slowly acquiring more land as he prospered.

Trotsky's formal education began at the age of nine when he was sent to a private Ukrainian-Jewish school in Odessa, Ukraine. It is said that Trotsky, at first, had some trouble in matching his peers at Odessa because his grasp of the Jewish vernacular of Yiddish—which was widely spoken at the school—was severely lacking. His Russian steadily improved, however, and soon he was well versed in Russian literature. Trotsky became an avid reader of Russian intellectual giants such as Fyodor Dostoevsky and Leo Tolstoy.

In 1889, Trotsky was transferred out of the private school system and directly into state-run Russian schools. He would eventually attend St. Paul's High School where he was considered one of the best students in the school, although he occasionally had some run-ins with some of his teachers.

Upon his graduation in 1896, Trotsky moved to the Ukrainian port city of Nikolayev, just off the Black Sea, at the impressionable age of 17. He had a couple of relatives that lived in this water town and decided to hole up with them until he figured out what his next move would be. Nikolayev at this time was a hotbed of revolutionary activity, and the young Trotsky soon became involved with the burgeoning scene.

He was at first against Marxism, but a fateful new acquaintance of his named Aleksandra Sokolovskaya would soon change his mind. Aleksandra, who was at the time studying to embark on the archaic profession of midwifery, was herself a rather unlikely radical, but she was six years older than Trotsky and already well-read in the typical liturgy of the leftist intellectuals of the day.

According to Trotsky, he was first drawn to Aleksandra because she was the first to outmatch him in a debate. He had met her among mutual friends when the topic of conversation inevitably turned political, and Trotsky was amazed to find that he couldn't beat the cold, tight logic of her arguments.

Trotsky recalls that he tried to point out certain inconsistencies he saw in Marxism, and he expounded upon why a unique brand of populism would be much more suitable for Russian society. But against her wit, his best-laid arguments seemed to fall flat. Soon enough—in the strange and classic way romance seems to be able to strike any one of us when we least expect it—Trotsky was smitten and found himself falling in love.

However, most of their relationship would have to blossom while Trotsky was in jail, after his arrest in January 1898. He had earned his incarceration by participating in a 200-strong demonstration of striking union members. This first arrest initiated a pattern in his life, and he would spend nearly two years in-and-out of jail before he married Aleksandra in 1900.

She, at this point, had been sentenced to four years exile in Siberia for subversive activities, and Trotsky went packing right along with his new wife. In those days, as cruel as the Russian state could be, it often deemed it appropriate not to break families apart and would send couples off to the frigid wastes together.

So it was that the newlyweds would spend their honeymoon years doing hard time in the cold, vast terrain of Siberia. The couple settled down in the Siberian village of Ust Kut. During their tenure here, this family in exile would soon grow to include two daughters, Zenaida and Nina.

By 1902, Trotsky was feeling restless, and at his wife's urging, he began to plot his escape. Aleksandra knew she couldn't leave with him due to her responsibility for their children, but she nobly encouraged her husband to make a break for it without her. This is a decision that most would be hard-pressed to understand, but Aleksandra was apparently such an ardent revolutionary that she placed a higher priority on the communist cause than her marriage.

Leaving with his wife's blessing, Trotsky made his way to the Irkutsk region of Siberia where he obtained a stolen passport. It was this fictitious name, hastily written on the pages of this passport as his new identity, that would go down in history as one of the primary leaders of the Russian Revolution. Taken in part from one of his jailers back at the prison camp, this little bit of spur of the moment identity theft would have Lev Bronstein forever known as Leon Trotsky.

Chapter Two

Trotsky Meets Vladimir Lenin

"England is nothing but the last ward of the European madhouse, and quite possibly it will prove to be the ward for particularly violent cases."

—Leon Trotsky

In October 1902, Trotsky arrived in London right at the door of the man who would be known as the veritable founder of Russian Marxism, Vladimir Lenin. It is said that for Trotsky and Lenin, there was almost an instant friendship. And regardless of the ideological differences the two would have over the years, Trotsky would remain loyal to Lenin until Lenin's death a couple of decades later.

In Trotsky, Lenin—who was ten years Trotsky's senior—found an eager pupil. Lenin set him to work, sending him on a kind of fundraising tour throughout Europe for the communist newspaper *Iskra*, which was on its last legs due to lack of capital. It was among the communist circles of Paris, France, while promoting this Marxist periodical that Trotsky met the woman who would become his second wife, Natalia Sedova.

Even though he never officially divorced his first love, Trotsky would marry Natalia in 1903. He has long been criticised for his abandonment of his first wife and children, but in his defense, some have pointed to his young age at the time and the uncertain conditions which made him believe he would never be able to see his family again. Whatever the case may be, he brought his newly minted spouse back with him to London after his tour of continental Europe came to a close.

It was in London in 1903 that Trotsky and Lenin both attended the Second Congress of the Social Democratic Workers' Party. This meeting of the socialist minds had originally been scheduled to take place in the future capital of the European Union; Brussels, Belgium. But with concerns of Russian spies in the region and a clampdown by Belgian police, the congress was moved to the democratic, ideological free market of ideas that London typically encouraged and allowed.

It is the irony which comes with democracy that England was letting these men, who would have gladly dismantled the British system, speak freely of their ideas under its very auspices. The main topic of discussion at this meeting was the recent split amongst the communists between the so-called Mensheviks and Bolsheviks.

The Mensheviks were the moderates who espoused a gradual change toward socialism and then ultimately communism. Whereas the Bolsheviks were the extreme hard liners, who wanted to bring about full and unadulterated communism by any means possible. The

Mensheviks eschewed violence while the Bolsheviks readily embraced it as a means to an end.

The more cautious Mensheviks, whose name translates as "Men of the Minority," were increasingly a minority among the group. And the Bolsheviks, or "Men of the Majority," were more and more calling communists to take up arms in a violent struggle against their capitalist overlords.

Lenin had advocated that after seizing power, the Bolsheviks should create a centralized power structure in which they could dictate to the common people of the proletariat. Trotsky was shocked and deeply dismayed by such notions, feeling that the Bolsheviks were calling upon a seat change from capitalist elites to communist elites controlling the masses.

But Lenin stuck to his belief that a group of centralized elites had to guide the people and reportedly told Trotsky quite simply, "There is no other way." Trotsky and Lenin left this meeting agreeing to disagree, but world events would soon shift the momentum into the Bolsheviks favor like never before when the first Russian revolution of 1905 broke out.

On the heels of a humiliating defeat at the hands of Japan in the 1905 Russo-Japanese War, the Russian state was standing on uncertain grounds, and the people in the street demanded answers. These sentiments came to a head on January 22, 1905, when hundreds of workers led by an Orthodox priest called Father Gapon led a demonstration at the gates of the tsar's Winter Palace.

Instead of hearing the concerns of his citizens, the heavy hand of the tsar decided to cut them down instead. A cavalry charge was ordered against his people, and artillery fire sent the mob running in the other direction as hundreds of their comrades had bullets and shrapnel rip through their bodies, leaving them dead in the courtyard of the palace.

It was a horrible scene to be sure, but yet many of the Bolsheviks upon hearing of it were giddy with delight. As macabre as it may sound; when the likes of Vladimir Lenin and even a young Joseph Stalin heard such news, they were overjoyed at the thought that the chaos and carnage would be the spark they needed to spurn on a communist revolution.

Trotsky for his part, unlike many of his colleagues, showed a much more human reaction to the tragedy. It is reported that upon hearing the news of the death toll among the demonstrators, he turned pale and even became physically ill. Nevertheless, when this tragic unrest evolved into a great strike in October 1905, Trotsky rose to meet the challenge.

He began to champion the cause of leading the formation of special workers' assemblies. These gatherings were arranged to create autonomous control of entire regions run by a workers' council, or as they were known in the Russian vernacular, a "soviet," which is Russian for the word "council."

The first council was created in St. Petersburg, Russia. Trotsky became the chairman of this soviet after the initial chairman, Russian lawyer Georgiy Khrustalev-

Nosar, was arrested in late 1905. The very next day, Trotsky's soviet was surrounded by tsarist troops, and he would be arrested as well, along with several other officials and dignitaries.

Put on trial by October 4, 1906, on charges of leading an armed rebellion, Trotsky stated his case before the court in what would be one of the most memorable speeches of his career. But all the exhortations in the world couldn't save the young thinker from being convicted and sentenced to a renewed exile in Siberia.

Chapter Three

A Prisoner of War

"Let a man find himself, in distinction from others, on top of two wheels with a chain—at least in a poor country like Russia—and his vanity begins to swell out like his tires. In America it takes an automobile to produce this effect."

—Leon Trotsky

Trotsky was being forced to return to the place he had so painstakingly fled from, but he wasn't going to go quietly. In January 1907, he managed to exact his escape from his handlers and made his way back to London, before moving to Vienna, Austria. Over the next few years, Trotsky would become an active member of both the Austrian Social Democratic Party and the German Social Democratic Party.

In October 1908, Trotsky was hired as an editor of the communist propaganda arm *Pravda* which had begun printing out of its Austrian outpost. Initially, the funding for the paper was very scarce, and Trotsky was eventually led to ask the Bolsheviks' Central Committee for more money just to keep the paper afloat.

After much prodding, Lenin finally assented to have the paper financed, but only under the condition that a known Bolshevik be placed on staff as an assistant editor.

As of January 1910, *Pravda* had become the mouthpiece of the entire communist movement. Trotsky would stay on at *Pravda* until 1912.

By 1912, the tensions between the remaining Mensheviks and the Bolsheviks had worsened, and Lenin led a charge to purge these meddling remnants of moderation from the party. However, Trotsky refused to be complicit in this separation, and in August 1912, a conference was held in Vienna in one last ditch attempt to heal the wounds that divided the communists.

Meanwhile, Trotsky continued to work as a writer for various publications, and later that year, he was sent to the Balkans as a war correspondent to cover the erupting Balkan Wars. He covered all the happenings in Serbia and Romania writing for the periodical paper *Kievskaya Mysl*.

Trotsky especially noted atrocities committed by the Bulgars, yet at the same time, he downplayed those perpetrated by the Turks. Interestingly enough, Turkey would one day prove to be a hospitable home for Trotsky, and one of his last places of exile before his assassination.

Shortly after his return to Austria from the Balkans, it would seem that the events that Trotsky had covered there as a journalist had come back to haunt him. A Serbian terrorist assassinated the visiting Arch Duke Franz Ferdinand on June 28, 1914; this was the spark that lit the fuse of what would become World War I with the Austro-Hungarian Empire declaring war on Serbia shortly thereafter. Trotsky recalls the frenzied mood of the Austrians at that time, with patriotic crowds gathering en masse screaming, "Death to the Serbs!"

It seemed the actions of one lone individual—who just so happened to be Serbian—enraged Austrians to such an extent that they were asking for nothing short of the entire liquidation of Serbia. In this upwelling of dangerous nationalist fervor, suddenly anyone who was not a native Austrian was viewed with the utmost suspicion. And Trotsky being a Russian national, whose country was historically aligned with the Serbs, wasn't going to fare very well.

It wasn't long before Trotsky was pressured to leave the country. He opted to move to Switzerland which was determined to remain neutral during the war. His stay with the Swiss wouldn't be long, however, and as 1914 drew to a close, he moved once again, this time to Paris, France.

From here he continued his writing, sending out vehement denunciations of a war that he viewed as pitting the common workers of the world against each other in order to do the bidding of their capitalist overseers. Meanwhile, the government of France had taken note of Trotsky's antiwar efforts and on March 31, 1916, had him deported as a result.

After being run out of France, Trotsky ended up in Spain for a brief time before the Spanish government decided to deport him to the United States. He was coming to the land with the motto of, "Give me your tired, your poor, your huddled masses yearning to breathe free, the wretched refuse of your teeming shore. Send these, the homeless, tempest-tost to me; I lift my lamp beside the golden door!"

Trotsky was indeed tempest tost and thrown out like refuse from most of the European societies he attempted to live in, now the only place he had to turn to was the magnanimity promised by the United States. Trotsky set foot in New York on January 13, 1917. Here he found a place in the Bronx where he wrote for local Russian papers, as well as the Yiddish publication*Der Forverts* or as it was otherwise known *The Jewish Daily Forward.*

Trotsky continued his life as a writer in New York City until he heard the tidings that Tsar Nicholas of Russia had fallen. He also received an official passport from the Russian consulate, signed and stamped by the Provisional Government that was temporarily overseeing all Russian affairs. Equipped with his new passport, Trotsky left New York on March 27, 1917, in an effort to take part in the drama unfolding in his Russian homeland.

He would only make it as far as Nova Scotia, Canada where the boat he was a passenger of was intercepted by the British navy stationed in Halifax. He was then detained at the Amherst Internment Camp in Nova Scotia, which served as a prisoner of war camp for the duration of World War I. Trotsky would stay there until pressure from the Russian foreign minister, Pavel Milyukov, finally convinced the British to release him on April 29, 1917.

After the abdication of Tsar Nicholas II on March 2, 1917, a provisional government had been established on a supposed neutral basis until a new government could be established. This temporary, provisional government was tasked with overseeing Russia's shift from a monarchy to a democratically elected assembly.

It was this hastily convened assembly that attempted to contain all the warring ideological factions, including the Bolsheviks, within its jurisdiction and oversight. It is with some irony that Pavel Milyukov secured Trotsky's release from a British prisoner of war camp, only for him to come back to Russia months later to help lead the charge to destroy the very provisional government Milyukov was serving.

Chapter Four

Putting a Stop to World War I

"The masses go into a revolution not with a prepared plan of social reconstruction, but with a sharp feeling that they cannot endure the old regime; only the guiding layers of a class have a political program, and even this still requires the test of events and the approval of the masses."

—Leon Trotsky

On May 17, 1917, Trotsky arrived in St. Petersburg, Russia to cast his lots with his revolutionary brethren. Among the intellectuals and radicals scrambling to get a toe hold in the ideological melee that Russia had become, Trotsky quickly became a favorite orator. He was invited to countless delegations, regiments, union halls, and even factories to speak before crowds who admired his rhetorical gift.

It was only on his second day in St. Petersburg that Trotsky had hammered out his famous three commandments, which he would deliver to his audience as the cardinal rules of the revolution. The commandments were: "Distrust the bourgeoisie, control our own leaders, and (have) confidence in our own revolutionary forces."

Positioning himself as the Marxist Moses, Trotsky at this point seemed almost destined to be a future leader of what would become the Soviet Union. Interestingly enough, in one of his many discourses during this early revolutionary period, he had set his scope beyond Russia entirely as he began to advocate for a "United States of Europe," basically expounding upon a communist version of the European Union.

Many have credited Winston Churchill as being the first to envision a United States of Europe, but Trotsky was arguing the same concept, except through different means, all the way back in 1917. But rather than the possibility of Europe uniting under one banner as the ideological dream Trotsky was imagining, World War I had Europe torn asunder more than ever before, and Russia was feeling the pressure.

Even though the tsar had been removed from the throne, the Provisional Government was locked in a struggle with the more extreme elements of the Bolsheviks who pushed for more change than the legislators in the Russian Duma (State Assembly) were willing to give. And after Trotsky took part in a pro-Bolshevik revolt in St. Petersburg on August 7, 1917, he was arrested and made a prisoner of his own ideology once again.

He would be released 40 days later, and once the Bolsheviks had become the majority of the city, Trotsky was once again elected chairman of the St. Petersburg Soviet on October 8. It seemed in those days that the winds of change could lock someone up one moment and then elect them as chairman the next; these were tumultuous times for Russia.

But by the end of 1917, the Provisional Government had all but failed, and in this topsy-turvy world, Trotsky had become the second most powerful member of the new Bolshevik state that emerged from the Provisional Government's carcass, second only to Vladimir Lenin. And when the Soviet leadership sought to negotiate the new Soviet Government's exit from the war, they turned to Trotsky, making him the People's Commissar for Foreign Affairs.

Before the Soviet takeover, the Bolsheviks' strongest rallying cry that brought them the most public support was their vow for complete withdraw of Russian troops from the trenches of World War I. The death knell of the Provisional Government was the fact that they had tried to continue the extremely unpopular war, which the tsar before them had orchestrated.

And now that the Soviets were in charge, they knew that in order to stay in power they had to fulfill their promise to the Russian people of a full withdraw, and they knew that the best mind they had at their disposal to accomplish this feat was the man called Leon Trotsky. Shortly after the Soviets assumed full control, Trotsky was sent to all the embassies in Russia to deliver the news that Russia was now a full-fledged communist state under the leadership of Vladimir Ilyich Lenin.

The Bolsheviks had hoped that they could convince the allied central powers of Germany, Austro-Hungary, and Turkey to agree to an immediate armistice. But hostilities would drag on until intermediaries, meeting in the Belarusian city of Brest-Litovsk, finally laid down their signatures on an official cease fire on December 2, 1917. And a few days later on December 9, peace talks began in earnest. Right on Christmas Eve, December 24, Trotsky arrived to lead the discussion.

At first, things appeared favorable for the Russians, but by January 1918, the Central Powers began to ask for some pretty heavy-handed concessions in exchange for peace. Germany, in particular, demanded that Russia give up any claim to Ukraine, Poland, Lithuania, and even parts of Latvia and Belorussia.

Although most of the Bolsheviks were appalled by such measures, Trotsky—ever the realist—knew that they didn't have much of a choice. The Russian soldiers' will to fight in the trenches had been lost long ago, and the exhausted Russian state, just recently placed into communist hands, would most likely collapse in the face of an invasion.

Although Trotsky didn't like the draconian measures dealt to them, he reported back to Lenin that the situation was dire, and Lenin agreed. He urged Trotsky to go ahead and accept the harsh terms that had been given. This sparked outrage and an intense debate among the rest of the Bolsheviks, and incredibly they managed to change Trotsky's mind.

Instead of accepting the bad hand that Russia had been dealt, he considered announcing Russia's intention to pull out of the war without signing an official peace treaty at all. Trotsky seemed to think that they could create a kind of de facto peace.

Believing that the war would end of its own accord, he explained to Lenin at the time, "We declare we end the war but do not sign a peace. They will be unable to make an offensive against us. If they attack us, our position will be no worse than now." Leon Trotsky would soon learn just how wrong he was.

Chapter Five

The Execution of the Last Tsar

"Life is not an easy matter—you cannot live through it without falling into frustration and cynicism unless you have before you a great idea which raises you above personal misery, above weakness, above all kinds of perfidy and baseness."

—Leon Trotsky

On February 18, 1918, an invasion force of Austrian and German troops poured over the frontiers of Russia in response to Trotsky's refusal to sign the proposed peace deal of the Central Powers. They found entire borders open and undefended and whole contingents were soon marching through Russian territory with virtual impunity.

Upon hearing the news, Trotsky seemed to be in a state of shocked denial and sent an official missive to Germany stating, "We request clarification of this misunderstanding." But the only misunderstanding that occurred was with Trotsky himself and not with the Germans.

Trotsky misunderstood how serious the Central Powers were and was bewildered that they made good on their threats of carrying out an offensive deep into Russian territory. At the urging of Lenin, Trotsky finally acquiesced and sent out an official cable to Germany the next day declaring, "The Council of People's Commissars finds itself compelled, in the present circumstances, to declare its agreement to sign a treaty on the terms proposed."

In other words, after Russian citizens found themselves facing down the barrels of German guns, Trotsky agreed to accept the terms of peace just as the Central Powers wished to impose upon them. The oppressive peace treaty was officially signed and ratified.

Shortly after this acceptance, Trotsky resigned from his post as Commissar for Foreign affairs. He then turned his attention to the incompetence of the Russian military and pushed for reform of the Red Army. He realized that the previous stripping of experienced commanders who worked under the auspices of the tsar had been a mistake, which had left the current army severely hamstrung as a result.

His views ran in opposition to many in his party, however, since they saw these former agents of the tsar as ideological enemies who should not have anything to do with the new army, let alone put in a position of leadership.

Nevertheless, when Trotsky was placed in charge in his next official role as People's Commissar of Army and Navy Affairs, he continued his efforts to reorganize the army and reintroduce more experienced candidates back into the ranks. Despite its criticism, this mobilization seemed to have transpired just in time to fend off a resurgence of the White Army opposition.

Trotsky was the commander in chief of the Russian armed forces, and he was ready to do battle. When he heard that the ancient Russian outpost of Kazan had fallen, he hopped on a train to survey the damage, but his train could get no further than the city of Sviyazhsk before they had to turn back.

Their rearguard was then approached by the enemy, and Trotsky's contingent faced the genuine threat of being surrounded. Trotsky's troops fought back, but all in all they would be marooned in Sviyazhsk for about 25 days before they were able to fight their way out. They had just barely avoided disaster, but for Trotsky, it was a victory; they had proven that they could fight back.

Meanwhile, the White Army and their western backers continued to show their dogged determination to roll back the clock of revolution and take back large chunks of Russian territory from the Bolsheviks. They managed to seize Vladivostok in the south east and essentially shut down the Trans-Siberian Railway.

And even more startling for the communists were the tidings coming from the north; the imminent invasion of a contingent of White Guard, bankrolled and backed by Western democracies, poised to seize Yekaterinburg. This was of dire importance since Yekaterinburg was the very city in which the tsar and his family had been imprisoned since his ouster from power.

This would-be rescue attempt, in essence, is what pushed the Soviets over the edge to sign the Russian royal family's death warrant. It was viewed as nothing short of an effort by the tsar's friends and family overseas to meddle and interfere with the course of the revolution.

And with these powerful backers on the verge of beating down the doors that held the tsar captive, it was decided that the entire royal family should be executed. Rather than have the embarrassment of them being rescued and used as a powerful propaganda tool against the Soviets, it was deemed that they should all be disposed of as quickly as possible.

So in July 1918, when the White Army was on the verge of overtaking the town of Yekaterinburg, the Soviets gave the order, and the tsar and his whole family were mercilessly wiped out. Almost immediately after their demise, the Red Army was pushed out of town, and the White Army did indeed arrive on the scene, but they were too late to rescue the tsar from his fate. Lenin was ultimately the one that had issued the order, and it remains unclear what Trotsky's role—if any—might have been in this turn of events, but he approved of Lenin and the other Soviet leaders' decision nonetheless.

Chapter Six

Russia Under Siege

"From being a patriotic myth, the Russian people have become an awful reality."

—Leon Trotsky

The year of 1919 was a bad one for Trotsky's Russia, and anyone on the outside looking in would have predicted a complete collapse of Bolshevism in a matter of months. The plight of the cities which faced disastrous famine was only outmatched by the misery of the rural territories that were engulfed in a virtual pandemic of typhoid, typhus, and even cholera.

The Bolsheviks had promised the Russian citizens land, health, and bread, and it seemed now that all they were left with was famine, homelessness, and disease. To make matters worse, the allied powers were waiting in the wings to swoop down on Russia's rotting corpse like capitalist vultures. All the while, the British and French blockade had completely sealed off Russia like a quarantined state of disaster, not allowing any people, goods, or even communication to enter or leave the beleaguered Russian borders.

Meanwhile, the military harassment continued with the Japanese threatening Russian borders in the east and rogue contingents from Czechoslovakia threatening rail lines in the Ural Mountains. There was also outright occupation taking place in the form of the British who operated out of the northwestern Russian city of Arkhangelsk, and German troops who were routinely patrolling up and down the Baltic.

These extraterritorial incursions were occurring right alongside the continued active warfare between the Red Army and their anti-communist adversary the Whites, who by October were at the very gates of St. Petersburg. At the approach, the local Soviet leadership seemed to collapse under the pressure and ordered an evacuation of the entire city.

Trotsky disagreed with this decision, and hopping on the very next train to St. Petersburg, he rushed to the scene to encourage the Red Army to resist. Under Trotsky's direction, the order to evacuate was rescinded. And instead, the city defenders dug in, bolstered their defenses with artillery placements and barricades, and determined to hold their ground.

Trotsky's dynamic force of personality seemed to carry the day, and his encouragement of the troops allowed them to muster enough tenacity to turn the White Army back, and the capitulation of St. Petersburg had been avoided. And soon after this victory, much of the momentum of the White Army seemed to have abated.

By 1920, the Russian Civil War was just about over. Sensing defeat, even their western allies began to jump ship, with the British leaving behind their occupation of Arkhangelsk, and the French evacuating their post in

Odessa. With the exception of a small holdout of fighters in Crimea, most of what remained of the White Army had been pushed out to Siberia.

But although the White Army had been defeated, the Bolsheviks barely had time to relish their victory before a new threat was on the horizon. This time, the aggression came from the newly independent state of Poland; creating tension and high drama that would eventually boil over into what would become the Polish-Soviet War.

Trotsky knew that there was no way that the Red Army would be able to put up a substantial fight against the Polish military, and he sought to have the Soviets sign a peace treaty with Poland. At first, however, these pleas were ignored and bloody battle ensued. Trotsky wouldn't obtain his permission to barter a peace deal until October 1920, which ultimately resulted in the signing of the Treaty of Riga, in Latvia on March 18, 1921. This treaty served to finally determine the boundaries that had been disputed between Poland and the Soviet Union.

With these matters finally taken care of, the nascent communist state had avoided its destruction. But in the next few years, the major problem with the Soviet Union wouldn't be of foreign invasion, but its own leadership. Lenin had suffered a massive stroke in May 1922, and an uneasy discussion of who would succeed him ensued. Many felt that Trotsky would make the right candidate, but there was an up-and-coming communist named Joseph Stalin who would beg to differ.

Chapter Seven

Stalin Takes Over

"The dynamic of revolutionary events is directly determined by swift, intense, and passionate changes in psychology of classes which have already formed themselves before the revolution."

—Leon Trotsky

Joseph Stalin had been made the general secretary of the Soviet Union in 1922. At that time, this post didn't hold much power; the general secretary merely served as a lead administrator who determined party membership, and everything the general secretary did was overseen by the Politburo (the executive committee). But Stalin, over the next few years, would do everything he could to expand the role and powers of this position.

Stalin would use this technocratic position as a springboard in which he could make fundamental changes to the party structure itself, and by the time anyone caught on to what he was up to, it was too late. In late 1922, Lenin had recovered enough from his stroke to address the issue, and on December 25, 1922, he sent a confidential note to the Central Committee in which he raised concern over who would succeed him in leadership.

This missive would become posthumously known as Lenin's will.

In this last testament of Vladimir Lenin, he sized up both Stalin and Trotsky, comparing their strengths and weaknesses. He declared that Trotsky was the "strongest personality," but he relied too heavily on unilateral administrative methods rather than consulting with other members of the council. As for Stalin, Lenin had delivered the ominous and prescient warning that Stalin had "concentrated immeasurable power in his hands" and should be viewed with caution as a potential successor.

And on January 4, 1923, Lenin made his feelings toward Stalin even more clear with a follow-up message, which regarding Stalin read, "Stalin is too rude and this fault, while quite acceptable in dealings between communist comrades, becomes intolerable in the office of General Secretary. I invite the comrades to consider ways of removing Stalin from this post and appointing somebody who is better in all respects than Stalin, namely one more tolerant, more loyal, more polite, more considerate towards his comrades, less capricious."

In other words, Lenin was trying to prevent someone he feared to be a tyrannical bully and despot from obtaining the highest seat in the land. By March 1923, Lenin was also exhorting Trotsky to do everything he could to diminish the role that Stalin played. Soon after, however, Lenin would suffer from yet another massive stroke, one that would eventually prove lethal, ending all further discussion on his part as to who should rightfully succeed him.

Meanwhile, Stalin had gotten wind of the fact that Trotsky was being groomed as a potential successor, and he began to do everything in his power to thwart that possibility. He began to actively campaign against what he called Trotskyism. Much of his criticism was aimed at the book that Trotsky published in 1923 called the *New Course*, in which Trotsky had advocated letting some of the old-guard Bolsheviks go, in favor of allowing a new generation of communists to lead.

Trotsky also maintained that the time had come for lower ranking members of the communist party to be given a fuller and more equal say, while other committees and secretaries (such as General Secretary Stalin) have their roles reduced in scope. This of course infuriated Stalin and led him to denounce Trotsky in stunning fashion before the Politburo, claiming that he was seeking to spread discord in the communist party by pitting the young against the old and the more experienced against the less experienced.

Soon communist newspapers were running anti-Trotsky articles that said—among other things—that "Trotskyism is an unnatural creation, the very antitheses of infallible Leninist Bolshevism and as such riddled with pernicious errors." In the midst of these new controversies and debates, Lenin passed away on January 21, 1924.

Trotsky's book was subsequently lambasted as being anti-Leninist and against party ideology, and copies of it were removed from public consumption. These open condemnations of Trotsky then culminated in his removal from the two offices he held as Chairman of the War Council and People's Commissar of War and Navy. He was stripped of these titles on January 2, 1925.

As a result, for most of 1925, he had found himself out of a job. But like any socialist state bent upon making room for everyone, he was recalled back in May 1925, to three petty new posts—all bureaucratically obscure—in order to occupy his time.

The three posts were Chairman of the Concessions Committee, Head of the Electro-Technical Board, and Chairman of the Scientific-Technical Board of Industry. Of these Trotsky quickly resigned from the two technical roles, citing interference from Stalin, but maintained his weak hold as Chairman of the Concessions Committee. But soon even his tenuous grip on this obscure office would slip from his grasp.

Chapter Eight

Trotsky's Exile Begins

"There is a limit to the application of democratic methods. You can inquire of all the passengers as to what type of car they like to ride in, but it is impossible to question them as to whether to apply the brakes when the train is at full speed and accident threatens."

—Leon Trotsky

Leon Trotsky was officially expelled from the Communist Party on November 12, 1927, and was exiled to Alma Ata, Kazakhstan on January 31, 1928. This was followed up by a complete expulsion from the Soviet Union in February 1929. Joining him in exile were his second wife Natalia Sedova and his son Lev Sedov.

The guards who escorted his family by train at first refused to tell Trotsky where he was being taken. Their grim silence had instilled the utmost fear and concern into the former revolutionary. Not only was there fear of the unknown, but also the very real knowledge that he had quite a few enemies lurking outside Soviet borders. He knew after his many years of fighting the White Army that there were many places outside the Soviet Union where his former enemies may attempt to exact vengeance upon him.

But no matter how fervently he asked his captors where they were leading him, they continued to refuse to answer him. Incensed, Trotsky committed himself to a hunger strike until finally on February 7, they informed him that he was being sent to Istanbul, Turkey. Upon hearing this, Trotsky was outraged and immediately rattled off a letter to the Central Committee, claiming that the president of Turkey, Mustapha Kemal, who was known to take a hardline against communists, would have him killed on the spot.

The Central Committee was unsympathetic and had Trotsky continue his journey to Turkey as planned. Despite Trotsky's grave misgivings, and the sense that he was walking directly into a Stalin dictated trap, the Turkish officials who greeted him showed him the utmost respect. They immediately found lodging for his family and carried his luggage with the care typically reserved for visiting diplomats.

But at this point—at least in the eyes of the majority of his countrymen—Trotsky was far from being a diplomat. The capricious whims and will of Soviet society had rapidly shifted against Trotsky in the last few years. And he was most definitely not leaving Soviet borders on a diplomatic mission but as a scorned political dissident and exile.

Realizing that he was not going to be immediately subjected to the firing squad, Trotsky decided to stay low for the moment and get back to his writing. He started sending out dispatches to his contacts in cities such as Berlin, Paris, and New York. Trotsky's leaked reports on his whereabouts and activity were then spread across all the newspapers of these major cities.

But even worse than this, his opinions and critiques of Stalin were openly presented to the world. In one article boldly titled "What is Stalin?" Trotsky launched an open tirade against the newly christened dictator, declaring, "His political horizon is extremely narrow. His theoretical level is equally primitive. His little book of compilations, *The Foundations of Leninism*, in which he tries to pay tribute to the Party's theoretical traditions, teems with schoolboy errors. He has the mentality of a dogged empiricist, devoid of creative imagination."

There it was; Trotsky the eloquent writer denouncing not only Stalin's behavior but his poor literary ability. It is incredible to imagine Stalin taking such stinging rebukes at all, and it is a true wonder that he didn't have Trotsky killed right then and there. But for the moment at least, Stalin didn't wish to show his true face. And it would probably seem too obvious, even for Stalin, if Trotsky had turned up dead shortly after such a public criticism. The whole world would assume that Stalin had executed Trotsky out of the anger that he had stoked. So instead of killing him, Stalin sought to stop the leak by putting Trotsky into further exile. Receiving commands from Moscow, Istanbul's Soviet Consulate immediately demanded Trotsky's removal and even threatened him and his family with physical coercion if they didn't cooperate.

He was soon shuffled off to the Turkish island of Prinkipo, here Trotsky would stay until July 1933 when

France accepted Trotsky's request for asylum. But although he was granted permission to live in France, he was curiously forbidden to enter Paris, and so he decided to live in the French coastal community of Royan where he was continually monitored by French intelligence agents.

Trotsky would stay in France until May 1935 when relations improved between the French government and the Soviets. The signing of the Franco-Soviet Treaty of Mutual Assistance persuaded French officials to call for the controversial former Soviet leader to be deported once again.

Trotsky then found refuge in Norway where he was invited to stay with the prominent Norwegian painter and journalist Konrad Knudsen at Norderhov. Trotsky and his family stayed with Konrad for a little over a year. Here Trotsky would write and have published his famous book, *The Revolution Betrayed*, in which he outlined—as he saw it—how Stalin had hijacked the Russian Revolution.

Trotsky would once again pay the price for his freedom of speech, and after being heavily pressured by Stalin, Trotsky was eventually deported from Norway. After being once again uprooted and removed, Trotsky would then head to what would be his final destination: a villa in Mexico.

Chapter Nine

Trotsky's Last Testament

"As long as I breathe I hope. As long as I breathe I shall fight for the future; that radiant future, in which man, strong and beautiful, will become master of the drifting stream of his history and will direct it towards the boundless horizons of beauty, joy and happiness! Life is beautiful. Let the future generations cleanse it of all evil, oppression and violence, and enjoy it to the full."

—Leon Trotsky

Trotsky arrived by an old steam ship at the Mexican port of Tampico on January 9, 1937. Trotsky received a positive reception from Mexico's President Lazaro Cardenas, who then put them on a train headed for Mexico City. Trotsky and his wife would live in Mexico City at the estate of a Mexican painter, Diego Rivera, and his wife Frida Kahlo from January 1937 to April 1939.

Trotsky became extremely close with the couple. In fact, he became so close that he ended up having an extramarital affair with Diego's wife. The house that the Trotskys were lodging in was Frida's childhood home, but it had been renovated in recent years and taken over by her husband Diego.

Frida's husband was gone a lot, and in his absence, Frida had become the main host for the guests and saw to their every need. But as she grew closer to Trotsky, the two developed affection for each other that soon went well beyond the normal between a host and a guest.

Affairs were not a new thing to Frida or her husband Diego, and at the time she was sleeping with Trotsky, Diego was carrying out a relationship with his wife's sister. It's hard to tell how much the affair bothered Diego when he found out about it, but he and Trotsky were already growing distant with each other and reportedly had a falling out over ideological differences. Perhaps the affair was just the straw the broke the camel's back.

At any rate, by April 1939, the Trotskys were moved out of Diego and Frida's house and into another house a few blocks down the street. His affair with Frida behind him, Leon Trotsky took the time to make some acquaintances in the local communist party, striking up friendships with notable activists such as James P. Cannon, Joseph Hansen, Farrell Dobbs, and Felix Monroe.

But as was usually the case for the life-long literary genius, Trotsky's passion once again turned back to writing. And it was from his new home that following summer that he delivered his most blistering attack on Stalin yet. At that time, the world was abuzz with news of the recent non-aggression pact Stalin had made with Hitler.

Trotsky knew that ever since Hitler's rise to power, one of Stalin's favorite charges to place on those he wished to be killed or exiled was to accuse them of collaborating with Hitler. So he was incredulous beyond belief at the apparent hypocrisy presented by Stalin's recent pact with Hitler. To see the Soviet leader openly working with the man he had so often demonized and used as a tool to demonize others was so patently absurd that Trotsky had to write about it.

And in the article titled "Hitler and Stalin," he described it as such, explaining, "Over the last three years Stalin has labeled every one of Lenin's comrades in arms agents of Hitler. He has destroyed the flower of the command staff, shot, replaced, or exiled around 30,000 officers, all on the same charge, namely that they were agents or allies of Hitler. Having destroyed the Party and decapitated the army, Stalin is now openly advancing his candidature as Hitler's chief agent."

Without holding back, Trotsky called it as he saw it, and with so few able to speak out at the glaring inconsistencies of Joseph Stalin, he was a much-needed voice of grievance and opposition to the Soviet dictator's abuses. Even so, Trotsky knew that after writing a piece like this, which so thoroughly exposed Stalin for whom he truly was, Stalin would stop at nothing until he was murdered and silenced for good.

And as if he sensed that his time on this Earth had suddenly grown very short, on February 27, 1940, Trotsky wrote what would be his last major work, fittingly titled "Trotsky's Testament." Similar to Lenin's last will, in this piece Trotsky laid down his final thoughts and feelings about the direction that world communism, and by extension, world politics were taking.

In this text, he vehemently denied that he had ever betrayed the Party or the working class, as Stalin had become so fond of accusing him of. After laying down his polemics and personal vindications, Trotsky then went on to thank all of his friends, and most notably his second wife Natalia who had stood by him through their plight as refugees, and—apparently—even through his sleeping around with other women.

He penned a whole passage about his wife in which he praised her, "In addition to the happiness of being a fighter for the cause of socialism, fate gave me the happiness of being her husband. During the almost forty years of our life together she remained an inexhaustible source of love, magnanimity, and tenderness. She underwent great sufferings, especially in the last period of our lives. But I find some comfort in the fact that she also knew days of happiness."

A few months after penning this testament, the seemingly prescient Trotsky almost lost his life in a raid on his house staged by the Russian secret police forerunner to the KGB: the NKVD. These Russian agents were successfully beaten back by Trotsky's guards, but not before Trotsky's 14-year-old grandson was shot in the foot, and Trotsky's bodyguard was taken at gunpoint and kidnapped, eventually killed by his captors.

After this attempt on his life, Trotsky wrote what would be his last article, the treatise appropriately titled, "Stalin seeks my death." Just one month later, on August

20, 1940, a man named Ramon Mercader would make that fear a reality. Catching him off guard, he came into Trotsky's study and struck him in the head with an ice pick.

The blow failed to kill Trotsky immediately, and the former revolutionary firebrand fought back with such ferocity that he managed to keep his killer at bay long enough for his bodyguards to rush into the room and seize the assailant. Surprisingly, Trotsky instructed his guards not to kill the man, contending that he needed to stay alive in order to stand trial and answer as to why he had attacked the exiled leader.

Trotsky no doubt didn't want the man who might be able to link the crime back to Stalin to perish. He could potentially serve as living evidence of Stalin's despotic corruption. Once the assassin had been successfully disarmed and detained, Trotsky was rushed to the hospital where he died a day later on August 21, 1940. He was 60 years old.

Conclusion

Leon Trotsky lived a life of intense thought and action. He was an ideological idealist, and like so many other tragic thinkers in history, he thought that he could change human nature with the stroke of a pen. Trotsky was the man that Lenin wished to succeed him, but for all his passionate idealism, Trotsky couldn't stand up to the savage realism that someone like Joseph Stalin presented. Stalin would forever crush Trotsky's dreams of a communist utopia.

But to be fair, you cannot say that Trotsky was just an innocent dreamer. During his years of authority, he had ruined quite a few lives on his own. It was Trotsky after all who abandoned his first wife and family to pursue his agenda. Trotsky also ordered executions, and when the shoe was on the other foot, he was not the least bit adverse to using torture against political prisoners. If he felt someone was obstructing his vision of how governance should be conducted, he wouldn't hesitate to take action. In the initial stages of the revolution, he even bore witness to his own father—a proud and successful self-made farmer—having his land forcefully stripped away from him during the agricultural redistribution process.

In the end, just like Lenin and Stalin, Trotsky was a revolutionist when it came to exacting a world and society that met his stipulations. To his grave, Leon Trotsky would never give up on his ideals, even after his motherland gave up on him.

Printed in Great Britain
by Amazon

28513392R00030